The Economics Handbook - A Primer on Economic Policy & History - The Greatest Authors & Books in Economics

By Commissioner George Mentz JD MBA CILS

All Rights Reserved 2020 Disclaimer for Mentzinger Media LLC

All works original herein except for economic writings from government websites in the public domain. Please consult a licensed professional before making any important decision.

First published by
Mentzinger Media, LTD

http://www.gmentz.com
Endorsed by the Academy http://www.gafm.com

© George Mentz 2020
The right of George Mentz to be identified as the author of this work has been asserted in accordance with the Copyright, Designs and Patents Act 1988.
ISBN – Disclosed on Publishing
ISBN - Disclosed on Publishing

Library of Congress Cataloguing-in-Publication Data
Cataloguing in Publication Data

A catalogue record for this book is available online

All rights reserved. No part of this manuscript or publication may be illegally copied, reproduced, stored in a retrieval system, or transmitted - in any form or by any means, electronic, mechanical, photocopying, recording and/or otherwise without the prior written express permission of the authors and or publishers. This book may not be lent, resold, scanned, hired out or otherwise disposed of by way of trade in any form, binding or cover other than that in which it is published, without the prior consent of the publishers.

Printed in the USA from Mentzinger Media, LLC USA

All insights or content in this document is information of a general nature and does not address the circumstances of any particular family, individual or entity. Nothing in the Site constitutes professional advice, medical advice, or financial advice. Please consult a licensed professional before making any important decision.

If you disagree with these Terms or are dissatisfied with this book or the author or the publication or publishing company, your sole and exclusive remedy is to discontinue using this book and its contents.

Contents

The Economics Handbook - A Primer on Economic Policy & History - The Greatest Authors & Books in Economics 1

Preface 5

The Greatest Books in Economics 9

1) The Gospel of Wealth 9
2) The Wealth of Nations Author: Adam Smith Published: Liberty Classics, 1776 11
3) The Principles of Communism 12
4) The Protestant Ethic and the Spirit of Capitalism 14
5) The General Theory of Employment, Interest, and Money 15
6) The Use of Knowledge in Society 16
7) Human Action 17
8) The Great Crash 19
9) Capitalism and Freedom 20
10) Out of Crisis 22
11) The Art of the Deal 24
12) The Competitive Advantages of Nations 26
13) Losing My Virginity 28
14) Irrational Exuberance 29
15) Straight from the Gut 31
16) The Art of The Start 2.0 33
17) The Big Short inside the Doomsday Machine 35
18) 23 Things They Don't Tell You about Capitalism 37
19) The Lean Startup 39
20) The Everything Store 41
21) Zero to One 42

22) How Google Works	44

Basic Economic Concepts 46

    Supply and Demand 47
    Interest Rates and Yield Curves 49
    Inflation 53
    Unemployment 53
    The Business Cycle 54
    The Phases of the Business Cycle 55
    Foreign Exchange Rates 56
    Financial Institutions 59
Glossary of Economic Terms 59

Author Biography 66

Preface

These are unique times. Presently in 2020, the stock markets are fairly high or have reached an all-time high. For instance, in the year 2000, we had a stock market crash where we lost five to nine trillion dollars in wealth in this country. People forget about it. It was 20 years ago. In the year 2000, the NASDAQ hit 5,100 and some change. It took 16 years for the NASDAQ to get back to where it was in the year 2000, all the way to 2017.

Economics has changed. A lot of these companies that didn't have earnings in 2000, now have billions in earnings. The NASDAQ and the technology market have continued to grow. The economics of the world has changed dramatically in the last 20 years. China is a powerhouse. India is growing, as are Africa and Arabia. South Asia, where Malaysia and Indonesia are, is also growing very, very quickly. The same goes for Latin America and Russia.

All of these different dynamics fit into what I would call a macroeconomic view. The macro view does change the way we think about everything. The stock market and individual investments used to be more reliable and more predictable. Since the 2008-2009 global financial crisis, however, when almost all stocks came down together, including the defensive stocks, people think a little bit differently. It used to be that people weren't thinking so much about gold, silver, and other commodities as a real, legitimate, long-term defensive investment. Now, people are looking at those things including crypto currencies, so you'll have investors buying stocks, bonds, treasuries, and even gold, silver, and other commodities, possibly including agricultural commodities. All of those investments are available today. If you go to an Exchange Traded Fund or ETF website and look at the different types of exchange-traded funds that are available, you can even buy funds that represent specific investments like cotton, copper, agricultural goods, or beef. I mean, there's a lot of different ways to invest on a global level these days.

From an economics view, then, you almost have to look more today than you did 20 years ago at the demographics of the world. I may have mentioned that only about 4-5% of the world's population lives in the United States. The rest of the 6-7 billion people are living outside of the United States. You have to look at those people not only as human beings but also as investors, stakeholders, and customers. If you're a company based in the United States, you can't put all your eggs in one basket and you must sell products and services anywhere you can legally.

A lot of companies are traded on the New York Stock Exchange, NASDAQ, and the American Stock Exchange. They do a vast majority of their business outside of the United States as 40% of S&P revenue comes from outside of the USA. That is what's happening. There's the United States, and on top of that, the United States is competing with 180 different tax regimes around the world. The USA is competing with 180 different countries that have sovereign laws, sovereign regulations, sovereign tax rates, worker benefits, and sovereign corporate tax rates. A US company may stay in the USA, but it also may pack up and go somewhere with better working conditions, better tax rates, and better corporate conditions that can help their company, employees, and customers and shareholders thrive.

When you look at an individual company, if you think in terms of "Business 101" and stakeholders, you're looking at the shareholders, the employees, and the customers. You're also looking at the suppliers. You're looking at the environment and the people around. To clarify what I mean by environment, it could be the local community composed of the people who live where the corporation is located. Those are the five key areas of stakeholders that you're looking at with regard to any company and its activities. Unfortunately, all of these 5 stakeholders have to cooperate—the employees, the suppliers, and the shareholders. Everybody has to cooperate because if one stakeholder of the five, gets too greedy, the house of cards can fall and the corporation can fail, particularly if the corporation is competing against hundreds of other corporations doing essentially the same thing in a more business friendly economic environment.

From the standpoint of economics, in the United States, historically we have only had a few traditional tactics to stimulate the economy. We can print money and spread it around, we can lower taxes, lower regulations, or we can lower interest rates for borrowing money. Those are three of the key areas.

We could also do something to help create jobs, which is the number one way to stimulate the economy. How you do that, though, is different.

Now, if you believe in Keynesian economics, you believe that the government has a key role in stimulating the economy through peaks and troughs. A peak is when the economy is up; a trough is when it's in a lower area and we may be struggling somewhat. That might be the time when the government decides to invest in infrastructure and start spending money on roads, bridges, schools, hospitals, and so forth. That's an example of Keynesian economics.

The flip side of Keynesian economics is Laffer curve economics. According to Dr. Laffer, if you lower taxes to an acceptable rate, you can create more paying customers for the government. They will be willing to do more transactions, more buying and selling of investments, buildings, land, and others. That's the Laffer curve effect. The Laffer Theory is also similar to the "Wal-Mart effect", as I call it. Wal-Mart is an obvious example that if you lower prices in an area, you can attract more customers when competing in your market. You have a lower or smaller profit on each sale, but in the long term you have greater revenue across the board for all the Wal-Mart people, shareholders, and employees. That's a little bit about domestic economics—the way the government has a role in it from the standpoint of interest rates, taxation, and regulation and some key issues with regard to global investing and global economics. From an economic standpoint, years ago, you could have a portfolio that was mainly just all-American goods, just solid American stock. You could probably still do that, but nowadays, it makes good sense to buy good positions that reflect the economies in other demographics.

You've got over a billion people each in: China, India, Arabia, South Asia, and Africa and half a billion in Latin America. If you can get your hands on good quality stock that does much the same thing as a successful company does here in the United States, it's probably a good idea to do so, particularly if there's a language and legal barrier against a US company going there.

I'm just giving you an example: If you liked eBay or Amazon as a stock 10 years ago, and you see an Amazon or an eBay price line style of stock in China, where a billion people speak Chinese and Chinese websites do a good job with online travel, flights, hotels, then you might want to buy the Chinese version of the stock. If you like what online universities have done in the United States over the last 20 years, you might like to invest in EDU/New Oriental Education, a diversified educational group in mainland China. It's trying to sell education and learning packages both face-to-face and online to over a billion Chinese speakers. This is an example of how the global expansion of ideas makes very, very good sense. The same logic applies to India, Arabia, and Africa.

You don't have to buy an individual stock if you don't want to. I mentioned before that you can buy a mutual fund or an ETF that represents various investing opportunities in specific countries in different areas of the world. That's just the basics of how global investing has changed. If you open an account with one of these stock brokerage firms, they might even allow you to invest in an offshore stock exchanges. Usually, investors just invest in the local markets and buy ETFs and funds sold within the United States. Sometimes, some of these accounts allow you to trade on the Hong Kong exchange, just to give you an example, where they have stocks that are specifically traded there. You might want to have access to buy one of those stocks, so you'd want to have access to that exchange. That's where the global economics is changing.

I remember visiting China several times in 2004-2007 and talking to leaders of the major banks there. Some of these banks I had never heard of before. The end of the story is that by 2007, about five of these China banks were among the top 10 banks in the world from a market capitalization standpoint, like China Construction Bank, Bank of China, or HSBC. Some of these banks are huge.

Global economics is changing. The world's getting smaller. The Internet has changed everything, and the technology and investing opportunities keep changing. With that, the opportunities for you and your clients have improved on a global level.

The Greatest Books in Economics – Summaries and Analysis

Here are short summaries and concepts from some of the top economics books in history. From capitalism, free markets, laissez-faire economics, to Engles/Socialism, up to the days of the Internet and fast moving innovation and creativity.

This book has 3 areas of focus

1. What is economics
2. Who are the top gurus, authors and writers in the area of economics
3. Basics of Economics and Glossary.

The goal of this book is to create a short handbook on Economics for VIPS and executives to review or for students to have access to an easy reference guide.

Below is information and takeaways regarding over 20 key books in economics over the last few centuries. We hope enjoy.

1) The Gospel of Wealth

Author: Andrew Carnegie **Published**: 1989

Best quotes or insight:

- "It is criminal to waste our energies in endeavoring to uproot when all we can profitably or possibly accomplish is to bend the universal tree of humanity a little in the direction most favorable to the production of good fruit under existing circumstances".

- "Great sums gathered by some fellow rich citizens and spent for public purposes, from which the masses reap the principal benefit, are more valuable to the masses than if scattered among them through the course of many years, in trifling amounts."

- "Those who would administer wisely must, indeed, be wise, for one of the serious obstacles to the improvement of our race is indiscriminate charity."

Summary Theme of the Book:

There are but three modes in which surplus wealth can be disposed of. It can be left to the families of the decedents, or it can be bequeathed for public purposes; or, finally, it can be administered during their lives by its possessors.

Key Takeaway or Best Tips:

The rich man should know that the best means of benefiting people is to extend the ladders upon which the aspiring can rise with: parks and means of recreation, by which men are helped in body and mind, libraries, museums, works of art, certain to give pleasure and improve the public taste, and public institutions of various kinds, which will improve the general condition of the people; in this manner, returning their surplus wealth to the mass of their fellows in the forms best calculated to do them lasting good.

Success Analysis

The Gospel of Wealth believes that quality work and perseverance lead to wealth. Carnegie based his ideas on the observation that the heirs of large fortunes frequently squandered their assets through disorderly living rather than nurturing and growing wealth.

2) **The Wealth of Nations** Author: Adam Smith Published: Liberty Classics, 1776

Best quotes or insights:

- *"Division of labor increases the productivity of workers; it allows each of them to focus on a skill and find innovative ways to produce a surplus."*
- *"The wealth of the nations is not determined by reserves of gold and silver, but its ability to produce tradable goods."*
- *"The desire of everyone to get paid for offering quality goods and services stems from self-interest, which inadvertently helps a nation generate revenue."*

Summary Theme of the Book

A free market, with limited government interference, minimized taxes according to income, and government protecting, building, and maintaining public works will allow buyers and sellers to choose what is best for them, thereby ensuring wealth creation.

Key Takeaways or Best Tips:

The government should step aside and permit the nation to prosper through a free market.

Success Analysis:

The government should protect the nation from violence, ensure the rule of law, and provide basic education. The first theme in The Wealth of Nations is that regulations on commerce are counter-productive while another central theme is that this productive capacity rests on the division and specialization of labor and the accumulation of capital that makes growth possible.

3) The Principles of Communism

Author: Friedrich Engels **Published**: 1847

Best Quotes or Insights:

- "Industry controlled by society as a whole, and operated according to a plan, presupposes well-rounded human beings, their faculties developed in a balanced fashion, able to see the system of production in its entirety."

- "Education will enable young people quickly to familiarize themselves with the whole system of production and to pass from one branch of production to another in response to the needs of society or their inclinations."

- "The general co-operation of all members of society for planned exploitation of the forces of production, the expansion of production to the point where it will satisfy the needs of all, the abolition of a situation in which the needs of some are satisfied at the expense of the needs of others, the complete liquidation of classes and their conflicts, the rounded development of the capacities of all members of society through the elimination of the present division of labor, through industrial education, through engaging in varying activities, through the participation by all in the enjoyments produced by all, through the combination of city and country – these are the main consequences of the abolition of private property."

Summary Theme of the Book:

The book talks about the conditions for the liberation of the proletariat (the masses). It talks about the proletariat about the bourgeoisie (upper class and industrialists), slaves, serfs, handicraftsmen, and manufacturing workers. The book was written at a time where there were still variations of slavery and economic slavery existing across Europe and Russia and EurAsia.

Key Takeaway or Best Tips:

An increase in the number of national factories, workshops, railroads, and ships bring new lands into cultivation and improvement of land already under cultivation; this is all in proportion to the growth of the capital and labor force at the disposal of the nation.

Success Analysis:

In 1848 Engels proposed that progressive taxation be used "to wrest, by degrees, all capital from the bourgeois, to centralize all instruments of production in the hands of the state."

The course of revolution for the liberation of the proletariat will involve limitation of private property through progressive taxation, gradual expropriation of landowners, organization of labor or employment of proletarians on publicly owned land, centralization of money and credit in the hands of the state through a national bank with the state capital, and education of all children.

4) The Protestant Ethic and the Spirit of Capitalism (1904)

AUTHOR: Max Webber PUBLISHED: Taylor and Francis E-Library

BEST QUOTES:

- "One keeps his commentary to himself at the sight of the sea or of majestic mountains"
- "The bourgeoisie and proletariat have always been and are affected by religion and upbringing"

SUMMARY OF BOOK:

In this book, Protestants believed that working hard has a duty and value for its own sake. Weber also defines the "spirit of capitalism" as a motivation to work and save money not just for survival, but in to also earn a profit. Through the book, there is an emphasis on hard work by Protestants which helped to shape capitalism as a lifestyle for generating profit for the sake of personal growth. He also argues that religious ideas such as Calvinism and upbringing by religious parents played a role in creating the capitalist spirit.

KEY TAKEAWAYS OR BEST TIPS:

Environment, upbringing, and your spirit of Capitalism affect the way you view material success.

SUCCESS ANALYSIS:

Since mental and environmental upbringing affects our choice of competition and occupation, to be successful, one needs to change his/her mindset and think holistically. According to Weber, the search for evidence of God's approval or disapproval led Protestants to see their business success as a sign of their devotion to God's expectations.

5) The General Theory of Employment, Interest, and Money. (1936)

AUTHOR: John Maynard Keynes PUBLISHED: By Palgrave Macmillan

BEST QUOTES:

- "Labor is always in a position to determine its wage."
- "What constitute the means of payment for commodities is simply commodities."
- "All sellers are inevitably, and by the meaning of the word buyers."
- "Everybody will bring a double demand as well as supply."

SUMMARY OF BOOK:

This book by the British economist expanded the view about macroeconomics as a central figure in economic theory. He also iterated that the way the government manages the economy could help the business cycle and balance the relationship between unemployment and inflation. He thoroughly challenged the highly held theories and provided an introduction to the application of Keynesian theory.

KEY TAKEAWAYS or BEST TIPS:

A government should always know when to make and how to make important decisions about supply and demand as it affects the welfare of Labor.

SUCCESS ANALYSIS:

- Government Intervention with good economic policies will go a long way.
- Keynes held that governments should increase spending and lower taxes when faced with recession or financial downturns. This should be done in order to create jobs and boost consumer buying power

6) The Use of Knowledge in Society

AUTHOR: Friedrich August Von Hayek - 1945

PUBLISHED: By Liberty Fund

BEST QUOTES:

- "Knowledge is key"
- "Knowledge... in the first instance is not given to the planner but to somebody else which somehow will have to be conveyed to the planner."
- "Everyone has knowledge. It is universal."
- "Practically every individual has an advantage over all others because he possesses unique information."

SUMMARY OF BOOK:

The book explains the importance of knowledge in a society which is disintegrated into two, the individual or unorganized and the authoritative or statistical or scientific knowledge. That knowledge, because of change in time and place, cannot be known to one single mind, and if it can be accessed from these two categories, then drawing up a comprehensive plan governing all economic activities would be less problematic.

KEY TAKEAWAYS or BEST TIPS:

Knowledge, though universal, can never be known and acquired universally by one person or organization but is disaggregated across individuals. Thus, planning and control over informational resources and assets must be decentralized where individuals can take advantage of that knowledge.

SUCCESS ANALYSIS:

The path of reasoning is diverse and spread at random to all individuals. To explore and exploit as much as one can glean is the path to economic success.

7) Human Action

AUTHOR: Ludwig Von Mises

PUBLISHED: The Ludwig von Mises Institute 1949

BEST QUOTES OR INSIGHTS

- *No economic theorem can be considered sound that is not solidly fastened upon this foundation by an irrefutable chain of reasoning.*

- *The logical structure of the mind is different with varying social classes.*

- *Man becomes conscious of time when he plans to convert a less satisfactory present state into a more satisfactory future state.*

- *People work only when they value the return of labor higher than the decrease in satisfaction brought about by the curtailment of leisure.*

- *Division of labor increases output per unit of labor expended. It intensifies the innate inequality of men.*

SUMMARY THEME OF THE BOOK

While a lot of scholars in the past have assumed that human action and reactions are unpredictable, this book seeks to inform its readers using economics, economic principles, and various government, producer, and consumer intervention to buttress its point that human action is a conscious reaction to its environment to satisfy his needs /desires. Human action changes when the society/environment/his condition changes.

KEY TAKEAWAY OR BEST TIPS

Freedom and liberty are not to be found in nature. A man is free as far as he can live and get on without being at the mercy of arbitrary decisions on the part of other people.

SUCCESS ANALYSIS

Human action is behavior that is purposeful where there is conscious adjustment to the conditions of the environment. Unconscious behavior are typically the reactions and the involuntary responses of the body and mind to stimuli. Science does not give us absolute and final certainty. It only assures us within the limits of our mental abilities and the prevailing state of scientific thought.

8) The Great Crash

AUTHOR: John Kenneth Galbraith

PUBLISHED: Houghton Mifflin Harcourt Publishing Company

BEST QUOTES OR INSIGHTS

- *One of the oldest puzzles of politics is who is to regulate the regulators.*
- *In the past, good times have given way to less good times and less good or bad to good.*
- *It takes more than money to control money.*

SUMMARY THEME OF THE BOOK

This book talks about the great crash that happened in 1929 due to the fall in the stock market. It gives a well-detailed insight of events that took place before the crash, events that lead to the crash, and events that happened after the crash such as the increasing rate of suicide among the Americans and the indifferent attitude of the Federal Reserve Board and the Federal Reserve Bank.

KEY TAKEAWAY OR BEST TIPS

The fact that everyone is doing it doesn't make it a norm. Do your research before diving headfirst into any investment opportunity.

SUCCESS ANALYSIS

When things are not right, rather than tell lies or sugarcoat the situation because you are afraid of public rejection. It is important to face the facts and be transparent in communications and seek solutions and tackle the problem head-on.

9) Capitalism and Freedom

AUTHOR: Milton Friedman

PUBLISHED: By University of Chicago press

BEST QUOTES:

- "It costs money to discriminate."
- "Economic arrangements play a dual role in the promotion of a free society."
- "Few of us would be willing to have issues decided by a bare majority."
- "A still more basic economic area in which the answer is both difficult and important is the definition of property rights."
- "If the argument is that we are too ignorant to judge good practitioners, all that is needed is to make the relevant information available."

SUMMARY OF BOOK:

Economic freedom is proportional to political freedom. The government should develop good policies but should also know when not to interfere with the flow of money in the country. Friedman also outlined that many financial problems such as the great depression were attributed largely to government failures.

KEY TAKEAWAYS or BEST TIPS:

- Keeping the political entities small and sometimes out of the flow of money will go a long way in protecting economic freedom.
- Economic Freedom and Individual Political Freedom are Related
- Social Welfare measures are a disincentive to the creative and productive powers of the individual.

- Progress via a liberated People, not by the burdens and control of governments

SUCCESS ANALYSIS:

Focus on aspects where there is a tradeoff between government or political involvement and involvement in the economy. There is little or no resistance to success there.

10)   Out of Crisis

AUTHOR: W. Edward Deming

PUBLISHED: Massachusetts Institute of Technology, Center for Advanced Educational Services, Cambridge, Massachusetts

BEST QUOTES OR INSIGHTS

- *The consumer is the most important part of the production line. Quality should be aimed at the needs of the consumer, present, and future.*
- *The wealth of a nation depends on its people, management, and government, more than on its natural resources.*
- *Most American executives think they are in the business to make money, rather than products and services.*
- *Measures of productivity do not lead to an improvement in productivity.*

SUMMARY THEME OF THE BOOK

It is a common notion in America that quality and productivity can be achieved by purchasing new plants, new gadgets, and employing more workers. Edward Deming was able to explain using Japan as a case study that quality improvement is majorly the responsibility of the management in a company, how well they can orientate their workers, and inspire them to buy into the company's vision.

KEY TAKEAWAY OR BEST TIPS

You can increase both quality and productivity simultaneously by using the same old plants and same old employees with a different orientation about what to do. Furthermore, using the same old plant and employees reduce production cost.

SUCCESS ANALYSIS

- The cost of renewing a product is only part of the cost of poor quality. Poor quality begets poor quality and that leads to lower productivity in the long run. More so, when poor quality gets to the hands of the consumers, it makes them unhappy.

- An unhappy customer is one of those figures that can't be known and likewise for the multiplying effect of a happy customer, who refers more people to patronize the company.

- You need statistical monitoring of quality to achieve improvement.

- Leadership should be focused on the system.

- Focus on quality first. Success will follow.

- "Drive out fear, so that everyone may work effectively for the company"

- Create a culture that balances safety and accountability.

11) The Art of the Deal

AUTHOR: Donald J Trump

PUBLISHED: Random House Publishing Group

BEST QUOTES:

- "Don't do it for the money, do it to do it."
- "Try to learn from the past... plan for the future by focusing exclusively on the present"
- "Most people think small because most people are afraid of success."
- "The difference between the successful and the unsuccessful is that the successful think big."

SUMMARY OF BOOK:

The book is about Trump's life beginning in Jamaica Estates, Queens. It then describes Trump's work in Brooklyn prior to going to Manhattan and building The Global Trump Organization. The book illuminates Trump's actions and thoughts in developing the Grand Hyatt Hotel and Trump Tower, renovating Wollman Rink, and regarding various other global projects. This book discusses how to always stay on top with your mindset. Always keep your momentum in the game; never let your opponent smell blood. If you ever have to think, think big.

KEY TAKEAWAYS or BEST TIPS:

- Think big. "I like thinking big,"
- Maximize the options.
- Protect the downside
- Know your market.
- Use your leverage
- Get the word out.
- Fight Back

- Deliver Value
- Have Fun
- Contain your Costs

SUCCESS ANALYSIS:

You are as big as you think. The millionaire does not do a harder job than you, he just thinks big. Therefore, to be successful you have to think big. Do not be afraid of success.

12) The Competitive Advantages of Nations

AUTHOR: Michael E. Porter

PUBLISHED: First Free Press Edition 1990

BEST QUOTES OR INSIGHTS

- A nation's competitiveness depends on the capacity of its industry to innovate and upgrade.
- Companies achieve competitive advantage through the act of innovation.
- Competitors will eventually and inevitably overtake any company that stops improving and innovating.
- Ultimately, the only way to sustain a competitive advantage is to upgrade it- to move to more sophisticated types.

SUMMARY THEME OF THE BOOK

This book studies and analyzes the patterns of competitive success in ten trading nations and was able to show that strong domestic rivals, aggressive home-based suppliers, and demanding local customers are all factors that pressure and challenge companies within a nation to be better.

This gives some nations the competitive advantage to compete globally rather than what was conventionally believed that labor, factors of production, interest rate or currency value are the factors that improve competitive advantage. The book theme is that the key to national wealth and advantage was the collective productivity of firms and workers and that the national and regional environment and assets supports output and competitiveness.

KEY TAKEAWAY OR BEST TIPS

Competitive advantage arises from leadership and management within a company that can take advantage, harness, and amplify forces to promote innovation and upgrading.

SUCCESS ANALYSIS

Innovation and change are inextricably tied together. After the innovation of a unique product that gives you or your company a global competitive advantage, you must make such existing product's advantage obsolete even while it still has such advantage and you build a better or upgraded version or else a competitor would make it obsolete for you.

13) Losing My Virginity

AUTHOR: Richard Branson

PUBLISHED: Random House Australia

BEST QUOTES OR INSIGHTS

- *You either go to prison or become a millionaire*
- *We would have about two seconds to say our last prayers.*
- *Success can take off without warning.*

SUMMARY THEME OF THE BOOK

Richard Branson explained with his life events that success is not just achieved in a day. He also showed his readers that irrespective of all the obstacles on the way, especially when starting a new business and getting discouraged by the society, at the end of the day you are who you say you are and your success is 100% in your hands.

KEY TAKEAWAY OR BEST TIPS

Risk and trying a new and alien approach to your business is the most important part of being an entrepreneur.

SUCCESS ANALYSIS

In Losing My Virginity, Branson illuminates the life events that shaped his youth and character. Branson's naivety, his sense of adventure, and his steely resolve led him to revolutionize the music and airline industries and his other businesses. Your risk-taking ability along with how you respond to devastating situations (e.g., panic during bankruptcy or building more strategies to come out) will determine how far you can go not just as an entrepreneur but also in life generally.

14) Irrational Exuberance

AUTHOR: Professor Robert Shiller - Princeton University Press

BEST QUOTES:

- "The reliable return attributable to dividends, not the less predictable portion arising from capital gains, is the main reason why stocks have on average been such good investment"
- "Most historical events, from wars through revolutions, do not have simple causes."
- "Those who know the ropes realize that today's hold recommendation is more like the sell recommendation of yesteryear."
- "The prominence of gambling institutions in our culture may encourage a speculative stance in financial markets."
- "Concentrate mostly on factors that have affected the market that is not warranted by irrational analysis of economic fundamentals."

SUMMARY OF BOOK:

This book does not bring a new economic theory or a work of econometrics but deals mainly with the cause and effect of fundamentals as it affects the stock market; this leads to the action that one might tag irrational Exuberance. This causes an overvaluation of a stock, which in turn just mean a burst looming as in the dot-com era and the housing bubble burst in 2007 and 2008.

KEY TAKEAWAYS or BEST TIPS:

- There is no more powerful effect than the Federal Reserve's chairman speech on economic fundamental analysis or interest rates as it can affect dramatically the value of stocks but sometimes the fundamentals are not to be trusted due to the flaws in data.

- The term Irrational Exuberence was popularized by former Fed chairman Alan Greenspan in a 1996 speech addressing the internet bubble in the stock market.

- Irrational exuberance has become synonymous with inflated asset prices and price bubbles, which generally crash, correct and cause major disruptions domestically and internationally.

SUCCESS ANALYSIS:

There is always a boom before a crash, therefore, to avoid the crash one should take note of the boom and watch it closely for unsubstantiated overvaluations.

15) Straight from the Gut

AUTHOR: Jack Welch

PUBLISHED: Warner Books, Inc., Hachette Book Group, 237 Park Avenue, New York.

BEST QUOTES OR INSIGHTS

- *There is no straight line to anyone's vision or dream.*
- *Differentiation is all about being extreme, rewarding the best, and weeding out the ineffective. Rigorous differentiation delivers real stars- and stars build great businesses.*
- *When people make mistakes, the last thing they need is. It's time for encouragement and confidence-building.*
- *For 25 years,* he said "you have paid for my hand when you could have had my brain as well- for nothing"

SUMMARY THEME OF THE BOOK

The story of the author shows that to manage and build a successful business, you must eliminate bureaucracy among employees in the workplace. Rewards must be given to the best team members because as long as you have the right people by your side and you make them feel wanted, appreciated, and welcomed, you can achieve anything you set out to achieve.

KEY TAKEAWAY OR BEST TIPS

- You have to think about the people and the quality of your products and services; you have to show your employees that they also matter and are the most important stakeholders in the company. If you can achieve this, success and profit won't be unpredictable.

- "If you don't know how to lose, you will never know how to win"
- Emphasize employability over employment
- "Never kick anybody when they're down"
- Create an organization without boundaries that communicates and absorbs information internally and externally.
- Everyone you meet is a potential talent or asset for your company growth.

SUCCESS ANALYSIS

The ability to work with people, reward them when they bring about needed innovations, chaste them when they do something wrong, and encourage those that are ready to learn from their mistakes is one of the best ways to be a leader.

Leadership becomes the willingness of those around you to engage your vision.

16) The Art of The Start 2.0

AUTHOR: Guy Kawasaki

PUBLISHED: Penguin Group Penguin Group (USA) LLC

BEST QUOTES OR INSIGHTS

- *Faith, not facts, moves mountains.*
- *Great companies began by asking simple questions.*
- *If we make meaning, you will probably also make money.*
- *Don't wait for perfection. Good enough is good enough*

SUMMARY THEME OF THE BOOK

This book is a collection of all useful tips required for a successful entrepreneurship journey. The book covers every area required for new entrepreneurs to be successful starting from how to come up with good ideas, how to lead a team to a common vision, how to grow through socializing and partnering, presentation of a business plan, the art of fundraising, bootstrapping, rainmaking, and more.

KEY TAKEAWAY OR BEST TIPS

- It is imperative that you first of all improve yourself, and then improve your team focusing on your strengths. If you do this, then your product will improve exponentially, hence, more revenue and profit.
- Create Meaning (create a product or service which makes the world a better place)
- Make Brand/Mantra (make a mantra out of your meaning)

- Get Going (start creating and delivering your product or service as soon as possible)
- Hire people who understand your product and are passionate about your product.

SUCCESS ANALYSIS

When you want to have start-up a business, you must conduct due diligence or a market survey and listen carefully to customers' problems. The primary goal of every new business should be to focus on building a good product that solves a particular number of problems in the society.

Much of the book is about doing a parabolic shift to "doing things differently, bigger, faster, and avoiding the undue middleman or regulations etc.

17) The Big Short inside the Doomsday Machine

AUTHOR: Michael Lewis PUBLISHED: By W.W Norton Company

BEST QUOTES:

- "It is laissez-faire until you get in deep shit."
- "You cannot tell someone that you asked him to lunch to let him know that did not think of him as evil."
- "... These personal foibles of mine were tolerated as long as things were going well. But when things weren't going well, they became a sign of incompetence."
- "I can only be as productive as my investors."

SUMMARY OF BOOK:

This book explains the conundrum and misconceptions that exist in the Financial, Bond, and Stock markets. It tells how different investors saw and exploited the facade the financial "masterminds"-as others view them- of the economy and society put up. Truly greed, corruption, and ego can be exploited.

KEY TAKEAWAYS or BEST TIPS:

- Greed, ego, and corruption exist and can be exploited. What moves the prices and how high they are placed in the financial markets is more than facts.
- Leverage can hurt investors and money managers in the form of defaults, overextended credit, options, derivatives, margin lending, real estate, etc.

- A weak chain link can affect almost every aspect of the economy. Different aspects of the economy

- Market optimism won't insure against a crash. Fiscal policy built on never-ending appreciation and

- Contrary to Gordon Gecko's sayings in another Wall Street movie, greed is not good.

- Investors should take care to protect themselves from risk. Even small investors at local banks lost big money on bond "mutual funds" that were loaded with junk.

SUCCESS ANALYSIS:

Find problems or flaws in the existing structure, determine how to milk it or avoid it, and repeat the process. This will go a long way in the journey to success.

18) 23 Things They Don't Tell You about Capitalism

AUTHOR: Ha Joon Chang

PUBLISHED: The Penguins Group

BEST QUOTES OR INSIGHTS

- *Free market policies rarely make poor countries richer.*
- *Markets weed out inefficient practices, but only when no one has sufficient power to manipulate them.*
- *Assume the worst about people and you will get the worst.*
- *Making rich people richer doesn't make the rest of us.*

SUMMARY THEME OF THE BOOK

Following the 2008 global financial meltdown, Ha Joon Chang was able to trace its origin to the free-market ideology. Although, he argues that in real life, there is no such thing as a free market. He was able to analyze the faults of free-market capitalism using 23 unique points alongside compelling research, statistics, and case studies. He believes in capitalism and he said it is best for every economy so long it is been bridled and regulated by fair government intervention.

KEY TAKEAWAY OR BEST TIPS

In reality, making a completely rational choice requires having all possible information and taking it into account the best possible actions when we look at all scenarios and alternative routes.

SUCCESS ANALYSIS

Capitalism in itself is very beneficial because people's desire to earn profits and money drives them to create new inventions for the betterment of society, thus making the society safer and healthier.

But capitalism must be bridled and a small amount of control must be given to the government to get a safer, fairer, and better system because fair guidelines and intervention from the government, who often knows more about the whole economy than individual companies, is more beneficial.

19) The Lean Startup

AUTHOR: Eric Ries

PUBLISHED: By Crown Publishing Group (U.S.A)

BEST QUOTES:

- "It is the boring stuff that matters the most"
- "What if we found ourselves building something that nobody wanted"
- 'Learning is the oldest '"excuse" in the book for the failure of execution'
- "Learning is cold comfort to employees who are following an entrepreneur into the unknown."

SUMMARY OF BOOK:

In his book, Eric puts entrepreneurs as the same as management, and throughout the book gives reasons behind every successful entrepreneur. He outlined all through this book that being a successful entrepreneur is more than just being diligent and hardworking; and being prepared in the right place and acting at the right time yields results.

KEY TAKEAWAYS or BEST TIPS:

- Success for an entrepreneur is in the process, not hard work and diligence. With the right process, you can save yourself unnecessary setbacks as an entrepreneur.
- Don't make the same mistake twice.
- New ideas and products will always be needed such as different services, products, approaches; management systems. Be ready to create !

- Keep seeking new ideas and solutions always !
- Measure and quantify things that can help you succeed better.
- Always seek to provide more value for customers with less waste or costs.
- Do only what is urgent, important and needed. Do what is needed to get to the next step or success.
- Seek continuous innovation.

SUCCESS ANALYSIS:

To be successful, you never give up as an entrepreneur. You never know what will work. Even a failed idea can product another opportunity.

20) The Everything Store

AUTHOR: Brad Stone : By Little, Brown, and Company

BEST QUOTES:

- "In the end, we are our choices"
- "Looking at things in new ways can enhance one's understanding."
- "Things don't just grow that fast."
- "When you are in the thick of things, you can get confused by small stuff."
- "It is easier to invent the future than to predict it."

SUMMARY OF BOOK:

Hard work and determination, the spirit of invention, and the drive to see it through are truly gems. Nothing is impossible. Start with a unique way of thinking and rewrite the rules day after day. In his book, he asserts that long-term thinking made Jeff stand out and his audacious will to do it made him implement the do-it-yourself principle that made the company a multi-billion dollar company it is now.

KEY TAKEAWAYS or BEST TIPS:

It is okay to have losses as a startup company as long as the losses will not chain your success but pave way for bigger wins. Do it yourself.

SUCCESS ANALYSIS:

- To be successful, never be scared to make bold moves. Use your imagination and tap into the unknown.
- Your customer service should know no limits.
- Don't think tomorrow or next month, think 20 years from now.
- DIY. Do it yourself and if you can build it better internally, DO IT.

21) Zero to One

AUTHOR: Peter Thiel

PUBLISHED: In the United States by Crown Business

BEST QUOTES:

- *"The true hero is the one that saves what is less important"*
- *"You don't have to fight, and when it is necessary strike hard"*
- *"People are scared of secrets because they are scared of being wrong"*
- *"If your goal is to never make a mistake, never look for secrets"*

SUMMARY OF BOOK:

Thiel exposes the evolution of his strategy in creating a startup. To create is better than to simply innovate others ideas. In the world of progress, creation is vertical and to innovate is horizontal. Monopoly and competition, the writer says, are the driving force to creation and innovation. Focus on creating your own value rather than mimicking others.

Peter Thiel is an entrepreneur and billionaire.

- In 1998, he co-founded PayPal with others such as Elon Musk.
- In 2002, PayPal sold to eBay for $1.5 billion.
- In 2004, Thiel was Facebook's first outside investor, buying 10.2% of Facebook for a half-million dollars.

KEY TAKEAWAYS or BEST TIPS:

- Monopoly is the best driver of innovations. Try to give value but most importantly gain value for yourself.
- Create a monopoly instead of competing with other businesses

- Control one small piece of the market share first, then expand
- The KEY sources of monopoly are: technology, networks, scale and brand.
- Emphasize distribution and sales from the beginning.

SUCCESS ANALYSIS:

To be truly successful, it is important to look at where people do not see value and create value. Add value to yourself first rather than adding more of what has been created.

Here are questions to ask yourself.

1. Do you have technological breakthrough?

2. Is this good timing.

3. Can you capture a market share

4. Is your company or team ready?

5. Do you have distribution channels?

6. Have you found an opportunity others have missed?

22) How Google Works

AUTHOR: Eric Schmidt

PUBLISHED: Grand Central Publishing, New York, Boston.

BEST QUOTES OR INSIGHTS

- *The most valuable result of 20 percent time isn't the products and features that get created; it's the things that people learn when they try something new.*

- *If I give you a penny, then you're a penny richer and I am a penny poorer, but if I give you an idea, then you will have a new idea but I'll have it too.*

- *Creative and intelligent people are the key to developing a great product.*

- *It is the ultimate luxury to combine passion and contribution. It's also a very clear path to happiness.*

SUMMARY THEME OF THE BOOK

How Google Works shows how Google's founds – Larry Page and Sergey Brin, and later CEO Eric Schmidt – created a culture that attracted top people, engineers, and employees who worked effectively to develop innovative products and services to become a powerhouse. The book talks about how a company's culture can attract people who are motivated and dedicated problem solvers and how it can also attract the best talent and inspired people, not just those looking for money. These cultures include natural interaction with colleagues, freedom for employees to speak their minds, and independence in decision making I.e., gives employees the freedom to make their own decisions and work on their passionate ideas..

KEY TAKEAWAY OR BEST TIPS

- Make sure you don't just hire creative employees; you must allow and give them the space and resources they need to task their brains and bring new things to the table.

- Smart Creatives are the lifeblood of Google. They are the employees Google seeks to hire. "Not every smart creative has all of these characteristics, in fact very few of them do. But they all must possess business savvy, technical knowledge, creative energy, and a hands-on approach to getting things done. Those are the fundamentals."

- How Google Works, page 19

- "[Everyone is] obligated to dissent if they believe something is incorrect or not in the best interests of the client. Everyone's opinion counts. While you might be hesitant to disagree with the team's most senior member or the client, you're expected to share your point of view."

- How Google Works, page 41

SUCCESS ANALYSIS

Build a company culture where nothing is based on function or experience but strictly on performance, enthusiasm, and the individuals makes the most impact. Eliminate bureaucracy and segregation and you will attract creative and intelligent professionals who will take your company to its peak.

As an important note on creativity, innovation and passion, Google staff are encouraged to engage 20 percent of their time at work on something besides their usual job description allowing the workers to expand on new ideas and solutions.

Basic Economic Concepts

Economics For The Wealth Management Professional

A key consideration before investing internationally is that the investor needs to apprehensively look into the prevailing international economic environment. The following economic principles will help the investor comprehend the economic environment before committing to a retirement or investment plan.

Gross Domestic Product and Gross National Product

Gross Domestic Product (GDP) can be termed as a measure of the goods and services produced by labor and property that is located in **a specific country**. For the purposes of the GDP calculation, it does not matter whether residents own the resources, it only matters that the labor and other resources are **located** in a specific country.

From an economic perspective, GDP is the most significant measure or international standard of national economic performance that is used by governments and economists worldwide.

The second key ingredient which commonly represents the economic power of a region or a country is the Gross National Product (GNP). A GNP is a measure of the goods and services that are produced by labor and property that is **supplied by residents.** It does not matter whether or not the laborers or the property is actually located in a specific country, so long as the resources are **owned** by residents. As there can be more foreign investment in various countries than there is in investment abroad, the GDP forms a larger chunk in magnitude as compared to GNP. As an exception, the GDP and GNP are nearly identical in the U.S..

A countries ability to produce is measured by its potential GDP. The growth in potential GDP is a function of the following:

- **The growth rate of the labor force-** The growth rate of labor force of an economy is defined by various demographic factors (such as birth and death rate, immigration, etc) and labor force participation rates (the percentage of the population that chooses to work).
- **The growth rate in the number of hours worked per worker-** The growth rate in the number of hours worked can be defined by a multitude of factors such as societal attitudes towards work and leisure.
- **The growth rate of productivity-** Productivity growth rate can be defined as a function of the technology used, innovation, social attitude, competition, resource utilization, and the skill of the labor force.

Supply and Demand

By definition the demand of a product can be calculated by the quantity of the product the consumers are willing to purchase.

Factors that affect the demand relationship of a product include:

- *The price of the product*. Generally, the price of a product is inversely related to its demand, the higher the product is priced, the lower the quantity demanded by consumers.
- *Consumer income.* In principal, higher the consumer's income, the more goods the consumer will demand.
- *The price and availability of related goods*. The demand for a product can be less if an attractive substitute product is available at a lower price.

- *Consumer expectations*. When the consumers speculate a product prices to rise in near future, the demand for the product shall increase.
- *Advertising*. Advertisement plays an important factor in promoting and escalating the demand of a product.. Proper use of advertisement can lead to an expansive growth of marketplace for an entire industry.

- *Demographics*. With the ever-changing demographics, consumer's tastes and demand change over years. This leads to the change in demand for products that the consumer effectively consumes.

The demand curve for a product clearly signifies an important correlation between the quantity of a product and the prices that would be paid for the same. The movement along the demand curve reflects a change in the quantity demanded. As a rule, when prices decline, the quantity of the product demanded by consumers will increase. This is called the law of demand, and it clearly emphasizes why the demand curves normally slope downward and to the right. When the demand curve shifts, this is known as a change in demand. Change in demand can also be caused due to factors other than the price.

In theory, the price elasticity of demand refers to the responsiveness of the quantity of goods that are demanded in relation to changes in the price of the product. Generally, most products have elastic demand. In principle, the demand is said to be elastic when a change in the price of a commodity produces a larger percentage change in the quantity of the commodity in demand. The elasticity of demand factorizes the availability of substitute products and the percentage of consumers' total budget that is spent on the product. For example, day to day necessities in general tend to be more inelastic than luxury goods. On the other hand, gasoline can be a good example of a product with elastic demand. Alternatively, some key products by virtue of their nature such as life saving medicines shall be in demand no matter what the price may be. For example, insulin which is used by diabetics. If the price of insulin was to double, in all probability the quantity of insulin demanded would remain constant. This situation can be termed as inelastic demand. The supply of a product is defined as the quantity of the product which producers or manufacturers are willing to produce and sell. ere is a remarkable difference in the change in the supply and the change in the quantity supplied. A **change in the quantity supplied** happens when there is a change in the price of the product. Consequently this change is depicted as a movement along the existing supply curve. Alternatively, **change in supply** occurs due to factors other than the price of the product. Graphically, a change in supply is reflected by a movement or shift of the entire supply curve up or down.

The factors that may lead to supply changes resulting in a shift of the supply curve include:

- A significant change in the price of essential inputs of production such as raw materials, labor or capital.
- Advancement in production technology such as the use of additional or more efficient machinery or production methods.
- Government induced changes such as changes in fiscal or monetary policy, imposition of taxes or other incentives or disincentives.
- Occurrence of natural disasters such as fires, floods, ice storms, or tornadoes which hinder the movement of goods on hand and may interrupt production schedules.

Profit forms a major determinant of a supply curve. As a result, a major factor that affects the supply curve is production cost. According to the law of supply, the producers will manufacture more of a product at higher prices in the short run, this leads to an upward movement of the supply curve towards the right of the graph. The main cause of such a relationship is due to the fact that companies will manufacture more of a product at a given price if they are able to cover the cost of production by selling the produce at a price higher than the cost of production which yields a profit.

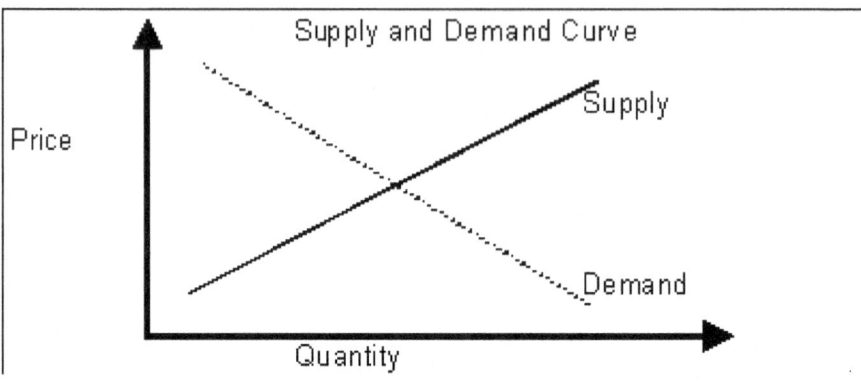

Interest Rates and Yield Curves

Quite interestingly, interest rates are a pivot factor which affects the securities markets and investments. Interest rates can be termed as a cost or price of money and can have a significant effect on the way a specific country's economy responds which is demonstrated as follows:

- *The cost of capital.* Impacts business investments and capital spending. As a result of decrease in interest rates, the business climate of an economy can expand by increasing the production capability and modernizing the existing manufacturing facilities due to cheaper cost of borrowing.
- *Current consumer consumption.* A regime of low and falling interest rates encourages consumers to spend and increase their current consumption of goods and services, particularly expensive goods such as automobiles and appliances.
- *Savings rates of individuals.* Rising interest rates may lead to more savings from the consumer's point of view which would also result in lowers consumption.
- *The discretionary spending habits of consumers.* As a result of increased interest rates, cost of borrowing increases which apparently increases the cost of debt servicing. Consequently, rising debt service cost means that there is less discretionary income to be used for current consumption.

The level of interest rates in a closed economy is a result of demand and supply of credit (loanable funds). A major supply of loanable funds is savers who invest their money, which in turn materialize into a loan for the consumer. The willingness to save is based upon the individual's willingness to trade current consumption for future consumption. The price demanded for this tradeoff is the interest rate. Thus the demand for loanable funds is a function of the desire for current consumption, the lower the interest rate, the greater will be the demand of loanable funds in the economy. Also, if the creditor believes that the rate of inflation shall be a key component hovering over the term of the loan, the nominal interest rate charged for the loan will be increased so that the debt will be repaid in real dollars.

Considering a free market open economy which engages in international trading, the level of interest rates, in addition to the domestic supply and demand factors just discussed, is also impacted by:

- **Central bank operations**. Central banks can significantly influence the short-term interest rates through money-market operations.
- **The foreign exchange rate**. If interest rates are higher in the U.S than the rest of its contemporaries, investment funds will flow into U.S (money goes where money grows), alternatively the government may force the central bank to protect the US dollar by raising short-term interest rates.
- **Central bank credibility**. If central bank of any economy has a policy to keep inflation under check, it can do so by having a regime of lower interest rates.

Graphically, the yield curve is a relationship that exists between the short and long-term interest rates which reflects different points of time over a business cycle. Any dramatic changes in the level of interest rates can lead to a change in both the price and demand of debt security. The bellwether that is used to establish the level of interest rates in a Specific Country's economy is the federal government's treasury bills (T-bills) and bond issues.

On a day to day basis, generally long-term interest rates are reportedly higher than the short-term interest rates. When interest rates are plotted on a graph against the term to maturity, the resulting depiction of the term structure for interest rates is known as a normal yield curve. When short-term rates are higher than long-term rates, the yield curve is said to be inverted. Quite often, the yield curve is inverted at the peak during an economic cycle. This is seen when banks manipulate the short-term interest rates upwards through its intervention in the money-market and other open market operations in an attempt to slowdown the economic activity.

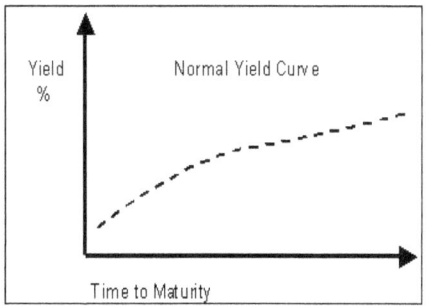

If you are planning to indulge yourself in the international trading in free market open economy, you ought to be wary of additional factors like:

- **Central bank operations**. Central banks can easily sway the short-term interest rates using the innovative money-market operations.
- **The foreign exchange rate**. If the US currency has high interest rates, the investment funds will automatically move into US market. Quite significant to note here is that money will find its way where it will grow. The banks, on the other hand, will react to the changed interest rates, as well as protect the currency by the process of increasing short-term interest rates.
- **Central bank credibility**. If central bank policy aims for keeping the inflation low, they will make all the efforts to keep the interest rates low.

The yield curve shown below clearly points out the comparison between short and long-term interest rates at different times of the business cycle. In response to changes in the interest rate levels, there will be quite a dramatic difference in the actual price and demand for debts securities. The rates for bonds, interest and debt instruments change in response to the costs of borrowing and the risk associated with government backed bonds being the AA> If you explore the usual and normal financial conditions, long-term interest rates are higher than short-term interest rates.

To know more effectively, you need to take a look at the normal yield curve, where you will find the interest rates are plotted against the term to maturity. The normal yield curve will seem to show inversion in the situation where short-term rates are higher than long-term rates. Furthermore, you will also find that the normal yield curve will also show the inversion in the economic cycle simply as a result of the Bank manipulating the short-term interest rates in the upward direction by involving itself in money-market and other open market operations.

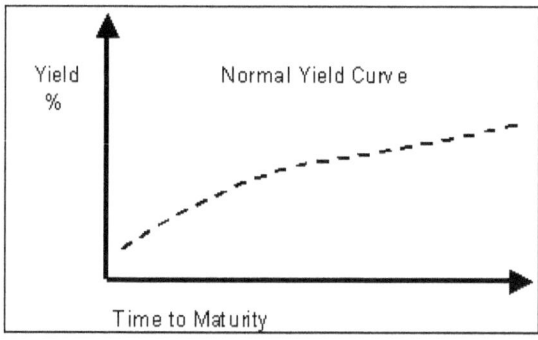

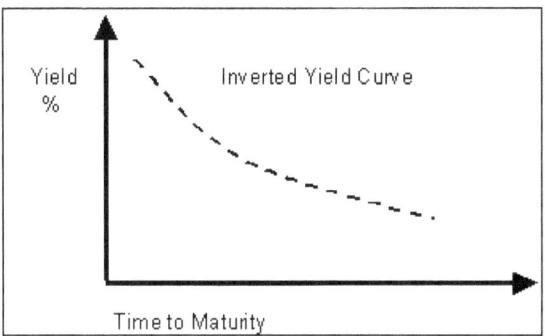

The term structure of interest rates is addressed by a variety of theories, which effortlessly make clear about the shape of the yield curve.

- **Segmented market theory.** This theory states that people who are investing in the bond market will essentially be concentrating their activities on particular maturity segments, which most obviously match their investment needs. Segmented market theory takes the serious view of shape of yield curve, it is based on the impractical supposition that the bond market investors will actually not diversify from their preferred segment, even when interest rate is low.
- **Preferred habitat theory.** This theory states that investors and borrowers would like to go for particular maturity segments which fall along the yield curve. The theory also clearly points out that investors would definitely like to deviate from preferred maturity segment (habitat) if they are satisfied that the financial risks listed by higher interest rates are manageable.
- **Pure expectations theory.** This theory explains that the yield curve will manipulate the participants' speculations on how the bond market interest rates will stand in future. In a situation where there is speculation of increase in the market interest rates, the yield curve will be sloped on the positive side. On the contrary, if the market speculations say that interest rates will gradually fall, there will be an expected inversion in the normal yield curve.
- **Liquidity theory.** The liquidity theory is essentially based upon the distaste of investors towards the risk. This theory points out that short-term rates should be lower than long-term rates and this would happen because the long-term bond rates should be inclusive of premium in case of absence of liquidity. In such a situation, the liquidity theory shows that the yield curve should always have a positive slope.

- **Biased expectation theory.** This theory is a perfect combination of pure expectations and liquidity theories. This theory would tend to explain in detail on the formation of normal yield curve shape essentially because of its liquidity preference, and its inclination to go for positive slope.

Inflation

According to one of the many perceptions and definitions of inflation, it is the constant rise in the cost of living. Consumer Price Index (CPI) is actually the best known parameter to measure the inflation on the basis of consumer goods bought in a month. This basket of consumer goods is essentially nothing but clear representation of the household goods purchased by an average family. As per CPI calculation, it is assumed that the average consumer is likely to buy the same type and quantity of goods every month or year, and the price of basket of goods is essentially predefined, measured, and compared for a particular base period. Besides CPI, settlements of collective agreements for unionized employees' wage demands is another significant indicator of market inflation.

The economic outcome of market inflation is very likely to include:

- The wearing away of the standard of living of people who live on fixed income resources.
- Beneficial for the Debtors as the loan amount is calculated and repaid with cheaper future dollars.
- High interest rates, which would ultimately lead into recessions.
- Gradual wealth transfer to the government sectors from the public sectors when the government is a major debtor, or when the tax system is progressive and not tied to inflation.

Unemployment

One of the objectives of economic policy is to create and sustain full employment. Here, the term full employment should not be taken as zero unemployment. If thought practically, there would always be unemployed persons to exist in the economy due to more than one known reason.

- Fictional unemployment refers to individuals who are unemployed as they are in search for the good jobs, but at present left their jobs voluntarily. There are certain demographic factors responsible for the change. For example, the young earning members will show high unemployment status since they search for good job prospects and lucrative career.
- Structural unemployment refers to those unemployed individuals whose specialized skills are no longer in demand because of socio economic changes

- as well as changes in the technology spectrum. For example, with the coming of the hi tech automobile industry, there were more jobs created for automobile mechanics and which resulted in horse carriage makers being put out of place.
- Cyclical unemployment refers to the normal changes in the unemployment rate caused by normal fluctuations happening in a business cycle.

The Business Cycle

An insight into the business cycle will eventually help the investor for focusing on the "Big Picture" to enable him or to gain a practicable understanding of long and short-term strategies. In general, the business cycle is one which is guided by seasonal variations, cyclical fluctuations, and long-term secular trends. It is also seen that the economy and business activity can be easily affected through the random and unexpected events like War, the "Asian Flu," or any kind of climatic disorder. While the long term growth of the economy has expanded and grown over time, there certainly has been volatility and periodic fluctuations. This periodic fluctuation is known as the business cycle. Quite significant to note here is that you do not have any specific parameter or calibration for the purpose of measuring recessions or dating business cycles. However, statistically, recessions are identified as two consecutive quarters of declining GDP growth. While different business cycles follow different kinds of business growth making each cycle unique, there are usually several businesses in the market that follow a fairly predictable pattern.

Irrespective of the fact that business cycles maintain their uniqueness in one way or the other, similarities and generic conclusions are deduced on the basis of business and economic cycles and investment strategies. Majority of economic indicators play decisive role in tracking the business strategies and phases of life.

Types of Economic Indicators:

- Leading economic indicators will predict the health of finance and economy. Some of the effective and leading economic indicators include building permits issued, housing starts, manufacturer's new orders for durable goods, stock prices, average number of hours worked per week, and commodity prices respectively.
- Coincident economic indicators such as GDP, industrial production, personal income, and retail sales will show the deviations in the same time and direction as you may watch it occurring in the overall economy.
- Lagging indicators such as unemployment rate, labor costs, inventory levels, and the rate of inflation alter course as the economy takes the turn eventually.

The Phases of the Business Cycle

The business cycle comprises four segments which can be recognized by the following signs or signals:

1) **Recovery and Expansion** - In this segment, the inflation is stable, or rising only to some extent. Typically, these stages last longer as compared to the contraction phase. This segment further shows that businesses are continuing to diversify their production line for meeting the demand of consumers. It is also seen that corporate profits show substantial increase and this could only happen as the profit margins are increasing. Businesses seem to be confident about making profits in the future and increasing the production. What's more, the new businesses are venturing and bankruptcies are slowing down. There is also an increase in retail sales and stock inventory is in control. Unemployment rate is also reduced and jobs are prominent and preponderant. There is a high demand for credit, besides consumer spending and housing construction, which will automatically increase economic activity. Optimism and confidence of investors increases which leads to a boom in the stock and bond markets. During the late stages of the expansion phase, the central bank will take on the measures for cooling the economy simply by increasing the short term interest rates. The investment strategies during the time of recovery and expansion are in gaining control over inflated common stocks because whole idea is to put an end to expansion.

2) **Peak** - Optimism and overconfidence take priority over carefulness and watchfulness. Stock market and other economic indices will show an upside above the long-term trends. There is fall in the profits, business revenue is slow, and the inflation rate is showing increase with enhancement in the wages. There is labor as well as product shortages on one hand, whereas on the other, speed of economic activity is high and the economic activity is slowly and gradually declining. Business revenues are down, profits are falling. Production costs are rising faster than prices, which causes profit margins to shrink. Business is no longer making large capital investment. Business output typically exceeds sales. Inventories start to build up due to falling sales. Accounts receivable begins to go up, which cause scarcity of working capital and this would eventually force the businesses to seek bank financing. Eventually, the confidence in business will wane. The confidence of consumer will fall, housing sales fall, and big-ticket consumer spending drops and more significantly, the consumers will start thinking on the future security. The investment strategy seen during the peak is increased stock selling in cyclical industries. Stocks show high P/E ratios, and low yielding stocks. Profits received in the rising stock market should necessarily be invested in short term investments like T-bills or money-market funds, and later earn from rising interest rates. Monetary policy will focus on tightening credit, and as a result the economy will witness a slow down. Rising interest rates will lead to an eventual fall in bond prices. Stock prices have destabilized and stock market movement shows decline. New stock and bond issues are rarely accepted by investors. Central bank will intervene for controlling the inflation and by increasing the short term interest rates. This would show inverted yield curves at this point of activity. Consumer confidence declines, housing sales fall, and big-ticket consumer spending drops as consumers worry about their financial future.

3) **Recession or Contraction** - In this segment, recession is evident and the economy seems quite unpredictable and melancholy. A recession or contraction phase is shorter than an expansion phase. Corporate profits are declining; business failures are amplify; industrial production is falling; and business confidence is getting worse. Additionally, there is a rise in unemployment; a fall in the consumer confidence; an increase in personal bankruptcies; and a sharp reduction in home construction prospects. Stock market activities decline and the

central bank is, by means of lower interest rates, encouraging borrowing for the purpose of increasing the economic activity. The investment strategy during the recession or contraction phase is to sell short-term bonds and to purchase mid and long-term bonds from which you would eventually benefit as a result of the lowered interest rates.

4) **Trough-** Basically, this phase shows the end of the recession time. Stock and bond indices are beneath the long-term trends. The rate of the decline of the economy begins to slow down. The leading economic indicators show sign of improvements and there is slow and gradual financial stability. There is plenty of labor; inflation and interest rates continue to fall; prices of raw material fall severely; low reduced personal income leads to reduced personal consumption; prices of raw material fall significantly; and there is a rise in the business and consumer confidence. In the Trough phase, the central bank is making all the efforts for increasing the economic growth by way of credit facility. Short-term interest rates are lowered in an effort to revive the economy. The investment strategy at this point in the cycle is meant for selling long-term bonds. Profits that one would get from long-term bonds should be readjusted by purchasing common stocks of cyclical industries which go out of place.

The Phases of the Business Cycle

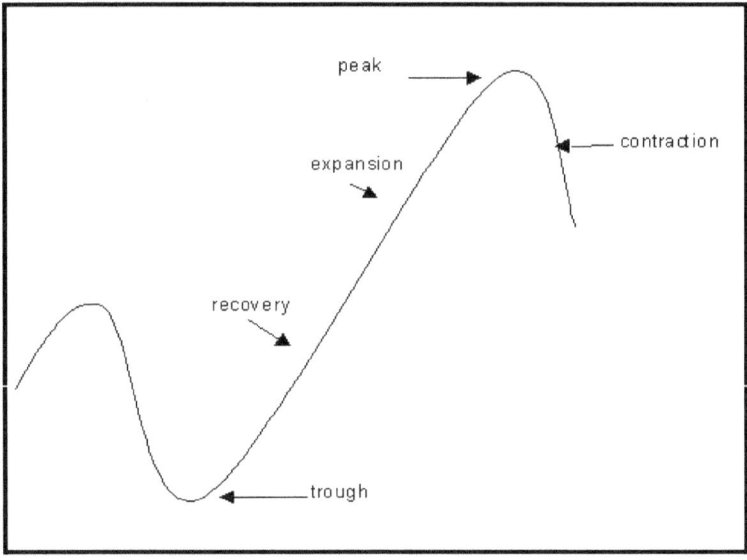

Foreign Exchange Rates

Global economic conditions have an effect on companies who sell their products into foreign markets, as seen during the times of "Asian flu" and the injury it caused to the economy during late 1990s. In addition, globalization plays a significant role in new competitors and trading partners.

Most countries' economies are directly dependent on foreign trade which essentially means that currency value will hold its purpose for people for earning their livelihoods. Quite important to note here is that the foreign exchange market is global in nature where currency trading occurs twenty-four hours a day. Additionally, in accordance with international standard conventions, all currencies are traded relative to the US dollar.

Internationally, all countries have the right to opt for either a fixed or a floating exchange rate system. A fixed exchange rate system is where the currency is hooked against other currencies. This is usually by stringent currency control measures which deter the citizens from holding foreign currencies. Otherwise, the central bank would ultimately take measures to make sure that the currency stays inside a fixed range by means of either purchasing or selling currency directly in the foreign exchange market. Currently, the classic example of a fixed exchange rate system is the Hong Kong dollar.

A floating exchange rate, on the other hand, would be controlled by the central bank in the event that the currency movement is excessive in nature. In such a situation, the respective central bank will either buy or sell the currency in the foreign exchange market. In the alternative, the central bank may manipulate the short-term interest rates. We have considered the US dollar to be free floating since the 1950s. In a situation where a particular currency is moving in a downward trend, central bank will automatically come into the picture where it will start purchasing their currency in order to increase its demand and strengthen its value. In a situation where the currency is showing weakness as compared to US dollar, the exporters will be benefitted substantially. Furthermore, the products manufactured in the U.S. or EU are costly when they are bought by the weaker currency. In short, when the currency is weak, the importers of the country which has a weak currency will be at a disadvantage as compared to the exporters of a country having a strong currency which in this event is U.S.

Factors Affecting Foreign Exchange Rate

- **Monetary policy**. An easy monetary policy will boost and contribute the money, and eventually tends to reduce the currency's exchange rate. A rigid monetary policy on the other hand will ultimately reduce the money supply and augment the exchange rate. It is the comparative monetary policies between two countries which explain the relationship between the two currencies. Hence, if we take a foreign exchange perspective, the monetary policy cannot be viewed as an individual entity all by itself.
- **Relative product prices**. If goods are relatively low-priced, they will always be in good demand. Purchasing power parity clearly points out that currency exchange rates regulate against relative price levels or the expected inflation rates of any two countries. Everything else remaining static, the country showing lowest inflation rate will get strongest currency.
- **Relative income levels**. If the income levels are on the high side within a country, its citizens people will be inclined to consume more and, as a result, they will desire imported goods. Therefore, the country that exhibits highest real growth rates show the weakest currency because the citizens of that country will spend a higher percentage of their usable incomes for imported goods.
- **Taste and quality considerations**. A country, whose goods are of high quality, or have high reputation, will be apt to have a quite stronger currency.
- **Interest rate differentials**. The country showing the highest real interest rate will definitely attract foreign venture and therefore strengthen its currency.
- **Relative profit**. A country that offers a high rate of return on equity investment, assuming equal risk, will attract foreign capital and thereby strengthening its currency.
- **Relative political risk**. A country that is considered to be a political safe haven will definitely attract foreign capital which will further strengthen the currency.

- **Currency speculation.** Foreign currency speculators will decide the supply and demand of a currency. These changes in supply and demand of currency will either strengthen or weaken the currency.

When we take the effect of each of these factors individually on the exchange rate, everything seems to be quite simple and straightforward. But, in the actual financial world, these factors put together will produce obscure results which make the dent in the economy.

Financial Institutions

There is absolutely no doubt that investment has turned out to be the real cornerstone that eventually helps in the process of planning and organization of one's finances. There are several types of stringent regulations and security laws available which provide a complete safeguard to the financial interests of the investors when they invest in their respective domestic markets. It is also evident that there are federal and provincial laws available which play a crucial role in the process of regulating the activities of investors.

NOTES

_____
_____
_____
_____
_____
_____
_____
_____

Glossary of Economic Terms

Agribusiness: A term that reflects the large, corporate nature of many farm enterprises in the modern U.S. economy.

American Stock Exchange: One of the key stock exchanges in the United States, it consists mainly of stocks and bonds of companies that are small to medium-sized, compared with the shares of large corporations traded on the New York Stock Exchange.

Antitrust law: A policy or action that seeks to curtail monopolistic powers within a market.

Asset: A possession of value, usually measured in terms of money.

Balance of payments: An accounting statement of the money value of international transactions between one nation and the rest of the world over a specific period of time. The statement shows the sum of transactions of individuals, businesses, and government agencies located in one nation, against those of all other nations.

Balance of trade: That part of a nation's balance of payments dealing with imports and exports -- that is, trade in goods and services -- over a given period. If exports of goods exceed imports, the trade balance is said to be "favorable"; if imports exceed exports, the trade balance is said to be "unfavorable."

Bear market: A market in which, in a time of falling prices, shareholders may rush to sell their stock shares, adding to the downward momentum.

Bond: A certificate reflecting a firm's promise to pay the holder a periodic interest payment until the date of maturity and a fixed sum of money on the designated maturing date.

Budget deficit: The amount each year by which government spending is greater than government income.

Budget surplus: The amount each year by which government income exceeds government spending.

Bull market: A market in which there is a continuous rise in stock prices.

Capital: The physical equipment (buildings, equipment, human skills) used in the production of goods and services. Also used to refer to corporate equity, debt securities, and cash.

Capitalism: An economic system in which the means of production are privately owned and controlled and which is characterized by competition and the profit motive.

Capital market: The market in which corporate equity and longer-term debt securities (those maturing in more than one year) are issued and traded.

Central bank: A country's principal monetary authority, responsible for such key functions as issuing currency and regulating the supply of credit in the economy.

Commercial bank: A bank that offers a broad range of deposit accounts, including checking, savings, and time deposits, and extends loans to individuals and businesses -- in contrast to investment banking firms such as brokerage firms, which generally are involved in arranging for the sale of corporate or municipal securities.

Common market: A group of nations that have eliminated tariffs and sometimes other barriers that impede trade with each other while maintaining a common external tariff on goods imported from outside the union.

Common stock: A share in the ownership of a corporation.

Consumer price index: A measure of the U.S. cost of living as tabulated by the U.S. Bureau of Labor Statistics based on the actual retail prices of a variety of consumer goods and services at a given time and compared to a base period that is changed from time to time.

Consumption tax: A tax on expenditures, rather than on earnings.

Deficiency payment: A government payment to compensate farmers for all or part of the difference between producer prices actually paid for a specific commodity and higher guaranteed target prices.

Demand: The total quantity of goods and services consumers are willing and able to buy at all possible prices during some time period.

Depression: A severe decline in general economic activity in terms of magnitude and/or length.

Deposit insurance: U.S. government backing of bank deposits up to a certain amount -- currently, $100,000.

Deregulation: Lifting of government controls over an industry.

Discount rate: The interest rate paid by commercial banks to borrow funds from Federal Reserve Banks.

Dividend: Money earned on stock holdings; usually, it represents a share of profits paid in proportion to the share of ownership.

Dow Jones Industrial Average: A stock price index, based on 30 prominent stocks, that is a commonly used indicator of general trends in the prices of stocks and bonds in the United States.

Dumping: Under U.S. law, sales or merchandise exported to the United States at "less than fair market value," when such sales materially injure or threaten material injury to producers of like merchandise in the United States.

Economic growth: An increase in a nation's capacity to produce goods and services.

Electronic commerce: Business conducted via the World Wide Web.

Exchange rate: The rate, or price, at which one country's currency is exchanged for the currency of another country.

Exports: Goods and services that are produced domestically and sold to buyers in another country.

Export subsidy: A lump sum given by the government for the purpose of promoting an enterprise considered beneficial to the public welfare.

Fast track: Procedures enacted by the U.S. Congress under which it votes within a fixed period on legislation submitted by the president to approve and implement U.S. international trade agreements.

Federal Reserve Bank: One of the 12 operating arms of the Federal Reserve System, located throughout the United States, that together with their 25 branches carry out various functions of the U.S. central bank system.

Federal Reserve System: The principal monetary authority (central bank) of the United States, which issues currency and regulates the supply of credit in the economy. It is made up of a seven-member Board of Governors in Washington, D.C., 12 regional Federal Reserve Banks, and their 25 branches.

Fiscal policy: The federal government's decisions about the amount of money it spends and collects in taxes to achieve full employment and non-inflationary economy.

Fixed exchange rate system: A system in which exchange rates between currencies are set at a predetermined level and do not move in response to changes in supply and demand.

Floating exchange rate system: A flexible system in which the exchange rate is determined by market forces of supply and demand, without intervention.

Food for Peace: A program that provides for the disposition of U.S. farm products outside the United States.

Free enterprise system: An economic system characterized by private ownership of property and productive resources, the profit motive to stimulate production, competition to ensure efficiency, and the forces of supply and demand to direct the production and distribution of goods and services.

Free trade: The absence of tariffs and regulations designed to curtail or prevent trade among nations.

Fringe benefit: An indirect, non-cash benefit provided to employees by employers in addition to regular wage or salary compensation, such as health insurance, life insurance, profit-sharing, and the like.

Futures: Contracts that require delivery of a commodity of specified quality and quantity, at a specified price, on a specified future date.

Gold standard: A monetary system in which currencies are defined in terms of a given weight of gold.
Gross domestic product: The total value of a nation's output, income, or expenditure produced within its physical boundaries.
Human capital: The health, strength, education, training, and skills that people bring to their jobs.
Imports: Goods or service that are produced in another country and sold domestically.
Income tax: An assessment levied by government on the net income of individuals and businesses.

Industrial Revolution: The emergence of the factory system of production, in which workers were brought together in one plant and supplied with tools, machines, and materials with which they worked in return for wages. The Industrial Revolution was spearheaded by rapid changes in the manufacture of textiles, particularly in England about 1770 and 1830. More broadly, the term applies to continuing structural economic change in the world economy.
Inflation: A rate of increase in the general price level of all goods and services. (This should not be confused with increases in the prices of specific goods relative to the prices of other goods.)
Intellectual property: Ownership, as evidenced by patents, trademarks, and copyrights, conferring the right to possess, use, or dispose of products created by human ingenuity.
Investment: The purchase of a security, such as a stock or bond.
Labor force: As measured in the United States, the total number of people employed or looking for work.
Laissez-faire: French phrase meaning "leave alone." In economics and politics, a doctrine that the economic system functions best when there is no interference by government.
Managed float regime: An exchange rate system in which rates for most currencies float, but central banks still intervene to prevent sharp changes.
Market: A setting in which buyers and sellers establish prices for identical or very similar products, and exchange goods or services.

Market economy: The national economy of a country that relies on market forces to determine levels of production, consumption, investment, and savings without government intervention.

Mixed economy: An economic system in which both the government and private enterprise play important roles with regard to production, consumption, investment, and savings.

Monetary policy: Federal Reserve System actions to influence the availability and cost of money and credit as a means of helping to promote high employment, economic growth, price stability, and a sustainable pattern of international transactions.

Money supply: The amount of money (coins, paper currency, and checking accounts) that is in circulation in the economy.

Monopoly: The sole seller of a good or service in a market.

Mutual fund: An investment company that continually offers new shares and buys existing shares back on demand and uses its capital to invest in diversified securities of other companies. Money is collected from individuals and invested on their behalf in varied portfolios of stocks.

National Association of Securities Dealers Automated Quotation system (Nasdaq): An automated information network that provides brokers and dealers with price quotations on the approximately 5,000 most active securities traded over the counter.

New Deal: U.S. economic reform programs of the 1930s established to help lift the United States out of the Great Depression.

New York Stock Exchange: The world's largest exchange for trading stocks and bonds.

Nontariff barrier: Government measures, such as import monitoring systems and variable levies, other than tariffs that restrict imports or that have the potential for restricting international trade.

Open trading system: A trading system in which countries allow fair and nondiscriminatory access to each other's markets.

Over-the-counter: Figurative term for the means of trading securities that are not listed on an organized stock exchange such as the New York Stock Exchange. Over-the-counter trading is done by broker-dealers who communicate by telephone and computer networks.

Panic: A series of unexpected cash withdrawals from a bank caused by a sudden decline in depositor confidence or fear that the bank will be closed by the chartering agency, i.e. many depositors withdraw cash almost simultaneously. Since the cash reserve a bank keeps on hand is only a small fraction of its deposits, a large number of withdrawals in a short period of time can deplete available cash and force the bank to close and possibly go out of business.

Price discrimination: Actions that give certain buyers advantages over others.
Price fixing: Actions, generally by a several large corporations that dominate in a single market, to escape market discipline by setting prices for goods or services at an agreed-on level.
Price supports: Federal assistance provided to farmers to help them deal with such unfavorable factors as bad weather and overproduction.
Privatization: The act of turning previously government-provided services over to private sector enterprises.
Productivity: The ratio of output (goods and services) produced per unit of input (productive resources) over some period of time.
Protectionism: The deliberate use or encouragement of restrictions on imports to enable relatively inefficient domestic producers to compete successfully with foreign producers.
Recession: A significant decline in general economic activity extending over a period of time.
Regulation: The formulation and issuance by authorized agencies of specific rules or regulations, under governing law, for the conduct and structure of a certain industry or activity.
Revenue: Payments received by businesses from selling goods and services.
Securities: Paper certificates (definitive securities) or electronic records (book-entry securities) evidencing ownership of equity (stocks) or debt obligations (bonds).
Securities and Exchange Commission: An independent, non-partisan, quasi-judicial regulatory agency with responsibility for administering the federal securities laws. The purpose of these laws is to protect investors and to ensure that they have access to disclosure of all material information concerning publicly traded securities. The commission also regulates firms engaged in the purchase or sale of securities, people who provide investment advice, and investment companies.
Services: Economic activities -- such as transportation, banking, insurance, tourism, telecommunications, advertising, entertainment, data processing, and consulting -- that normally are consumed as they are produced, as contrasted with economic goods, which are more tangible.
Socialism: An economic system in which the basic means of production are primarily owned and controlled collectively, usually by government under some system of central planning.

Social regulation: Government-imposed restrictions designed to discourage or prohibit harmful corporate behavior (such as polluting the environment or putting workers in dangerous work situations) or to encourage behavior deemed socially desirable.

Social Security: A U.S. government pension program that provides benefits to retirees based on their own and their employers' contributions to the program while they were working.

Standard of living: A minimum of necessities, comforts, or luxuries considered essential to maintaining a person or group in customary or proper status or circumstances.

Stagflation: An economic condition of both continuing inflation and stagnant business activity.

Stock: Ownership shares in the assets of a corporation.

Stock exchange: An organized market for the buying and selling of stocks and bonds.

Subsidy: An economic benefit, direct or indirect, granted by a government to domestic producers of goods or services, often to strengthen their competitive position against foreign companies.

Supply: A schedule of how much producers are willing and able to sell at all possible prices during some time period.

Tariff: A duty levied on goods transported from one customs area to another either for protective or revenue purposes.

Trade deficit: The amount by which a country's merchandise exports exceed its merchandise imports.

Trade surplus: The amount by which a country's merchandise exports exceed its imports.

Venture capital: Investment in a new, generally possibly risky, enterprise.

Author Biography

Commissioner George Mentz JD MBA CILS is a global entrepreneur trained in international law who has worked or traveled in over 40 nations worldwide. Mentz is an international award winning author and educator based in the United States. Mentz is the first business and law professor in the USA to be multi credentialed in: international law, management consulting, wealth management/financial consulting, and financial planning along with having an earned MBA and JD/Doctor of Jurisprudence degree and US law license.

Counselor Mentz is one of the few JD/MBA holders in the USA to earn a CILS Graduate Cert./Diploma in International Legal Studies. Mentz is the Titular Seigneur of the Feif of Blondel in Guernsey which is a legally registered Fief that is over 700 years old. Mentz is a US Commissioner for the White House Presidential Scholars Program in the USA. Mentz received his DSS Doctor of Spiritual Studies from the Emerson Institute and is a Member of the ANTN Affiliated New Thought Network. Mentz established the Global Association for the Chartered Economist ® and educational programs in the USA, EU and Africa that are offered worldwide.

This is a first of its kind primer on economic and business philosophy. The book discusses many of the great gurus of economics and finance. The manuscript contains much historical information in international business and economic policy. The book has key information top themes and ideas of the greatest philosophers in economics and business over the centuries up till the present day along with the basics of the US Economic System.
www.gmentz.com

www.ingramcontent.com/pod-product-compliance
Lightning Source LLC
Chambersburg PA
CBHW070500220526
45466CB00004B/1904